The Simple Life

Other Books By The Author

The Shooting Salvationist
Camelot's Cousin
November Surprise
In the Arena
Capitol Limited
Jake & Clara
How to Keep Calm & Carry On

The Simple Life
Reflections on the Twenty-Third Psalm

David R. Stokes

Copyright 2015 David R. Stokes

Critical Mass Press
Fairfax, Virginia

ISBN 978-0-9969892-2-0 (soft cover)
ISBN 978-0-9969892-3-7 (ebook)

Cover Design by Michael Zizolfo
Interior Design by Penoaks Publishing, http://penoaks.com

For more information, visit the author's website:
www.davidrstokes.com

All scripture references in this book, unless otherwise indicated, are from the New International Version (copyright © 1973, 1978, 1984 by International Bible Society). When other translations are cited, the following initials are used: KJV (King James Version), NKJV (New King James Version), and NLT (New Living Translation).

Dedication

To MARY WHITE. Goodness and mercy followed her all the days of her life, and she dwells in the house of the Lord forever.

"The most valuable thing the Psalms do for me is to express the same delight in God which made David dance."

— *C.S. Lewis*

Chapter One
Supernatural Stress Relief

LIFE GETS COMPLICATED. Sometimes we're pre–*trib*, other times we're mid–*trib*, and even post–*trib*. You may think I'm talking about ideas as to the timing of the rapture in Biblical prophecy, but I'm not.

Stay with me.

I'm talking about trial and trouble. That kind of *tribulation*. Some reading this are just beginning to face trouble. Others of you may be smack dab in the middle of a big mess. And maybe some of you have just emerged from a painful episode in your life. That's the nature of life. I don't know if we fully grasp that. We think there's going to be some point when God is going to love us so much better than everybody else that He is going to make it so we get to skip some of the bad stuff.

But it doesn't work that way.

The Simple Life

This book is about the twenty–third Psalm, and we begin with a look at *Supernatural Stress Relief*. God has not promised us a life without problems, pain, or stress. But there is a way to navigate troubled waters. In fact, that's the greater testimony. The greater witness before the world is not, "Look at that person. They have no problems. I wonder what their secret is"—because there are no people like that. The real witness comes when people say, "Look at that person who is having such difficult problems and doesn't seem to be as rattled as I would be." That's when people come to us for answers.

David wrote the famous Psalm. He was the king of Israel. Before that, he was a shepherd. His family was in the sheep business.

All Scripture is given by inspiration of God, God–breathed. It was written to a world that is a little foreign to us, because we're industrial. We're technological. But the great driving force in economies prior to the Industrial Age was agriculture. Everything was based on that. That's why there are so many herding and farming references and metaphors in the Bible.

In fact, the chosen metaphor God uses for the people who follow him is to describe us as sheep of His pasture. Therefore, we need a shepherd. David himself was involved in that family business.

Some people think, "Well, he must have written this during the downtime out in the fields." But that's not when he wrote it. There's too much in the psalm that tells us David was much older and had more experience. He talks about enemies. He talks about the valley of the shadow of death.

Most students of the Bible who have researched this agree that the most likely period of time for David to write this Psalm was when he was in his fifties. He was experiencing a tumultuous period in his kingdom. His son Absalom was leading a revolt, and many of his key people, including his chief of staff, had betrayed him in political revolt. David was literally running for his life.

It's against this backdrop that David went back in his mind to his time as a shepherd boy and the precious time he spent with God. Even after he was told by the man of God, "He is going to be the next king of Israel," he still had to go out and tend the sheep.

He went back to that time when life was much less stressful and complicated. He didn't have to worry about a nation. He didn't have to worry about political threats. Sheep were not attack animals. He was living *the simple life*.

The twenty–third Psalm is not just something to be read ceremoniously at funerals, it's something for us *now*— everyday. It's a powerful creed. It's a powerful way to live.

I have a hard time relating to the idea of shepherds and the sheep except in the pastoral sense. The word *pastor* means shepherd. God was speaking to David using the narrative of his life and the experiences and the skills of the pasture. God loves to use our narrative to reveal His purposes.

From what I know about shepherding sheep in a field, it's pretty mundane work. But when you relate even the mundane to God, it comes alive. That's what David learned to do.

There are two thoughts in Psalm 23:1. They're independent clauses separated by a semicolon: *"The Lord is my shepherd; I shall not want."*

They are connected and related. You can't understand one without the other. If you find yourself falling short in the, *"...I shall not want"* part, then something is wrong in your application of the *"Shepherd"* part.

Let's take it apart even more. Start with the simple statement: *"The Lord is..."*

David believed there is a God. I love that line from the movie from the 1990s, *Rudy*, about the guy who always wanted to play for Notre Dame. He went to a priest to talk about God. The cleric said something brilliant: "I've studied theology for all of my life, and there are only two incontrovertible truths I've learned. The first is there is a God, and the second is I am not Him."

In theology, you learn about the ontological arguments for God, the teleological arguments for God, the cosmological arguments for God, and the anthropological arguments for

David R. Stokes

God. That's all fine and good, but David is not interested in mere theology, he is interested in relating his life to something bigger than himself.

"The Lord is…"

He believed in God. I understand there is great discussion among people in the world about creationism, intelligent design, and such things, but the way I resolved that in my heart and mind as a young man was not with the question, "did God create the heavens and the earth?" But rather, I asked, "*could* God create the heavens and the earth?" If I believe in a great, transcendent, almighty, powerful God who *could*, it's a small step to say he *did*. If somebody is saying he *didn't*, what they're really saying is he *couldn't*.

There is this tremendous effort on the part of humanity and even some who speak in the name of religion to bring God down and somehow accommodate God to whatever thinking happens to be popular in the world at that particular moment. I recently re-read a book written by Billy Graham, in 1965, called "World Aflame." I was amazed at how it spoke to life in the 21st century even though it was penned more than 50 years ago. In the introduction, Graham said this:

"As a Christian, I am under no obligation to attempt to reconcile the Bible's teachings with modern philosophy. Biblical truth does not parallel human opinion of any generation; it usually opposes it! We are to be witnesses, not imitators. The prophets who spoke to their generations for God did not please and conform; they irritated and

opposed. The Bible's philosophy of man in history begins with God as the Creator of the universe. The Bible presents man as being in rebellion against God. This began when, in an overt act of self-will, our first parents rebelled against divine law. In this experience man ruined his divine image, became alienated from God, and started on a course of action that produced civilizations and cultures saturated with crime, lust, hate, greed, and war. The earth is a planet in rebellion."

"The Lord is…"

Hebrews 11:6 (NIV) reminds us: *"But without faith it is impossible to please Him…"* That's God. *"…for he who comes to God must believe that He is, and that He is a rewarder of those who diligently seek Him."*

You may say, "Well, I don't know if I believe in God or not." All right. I'm going to give you an exercise. I want you to honestly and sincerely find a quiet place and think this through. And if you're not sure that you believe in God, pray a prayer like this: *"If you are real, God, I am seeking to know you with all my heart. I really want the answer. If you are real, please show me and make yourself real to me."*

I believe with all my heart that anytime a prayer like that is prayed anywhere on this planet, God delights to answer. He will answer that prayer. It's not just a matter of seek and you will find. In a real sense, if you seek God, He will find you.

"The Lord is…"

David R. Stokes

There is a God. Proverbs 29:18 (NIV) says, *"Where there is no revelation, people cast off restraint..."*

In the world in which we live today, people are moving away from a belief in Almighty God and dumbing God down. The Russian novelist, Fyodor Dostoyevsky, wrote: "If there is no God, everything is permissible." We see evidence of this all around us today.

David's Psalm will not comfort you until you begin with— *"The Lord is..."*

Next, David reminds us that the Lord is a *shepherd*. Again, he is talking about his own experience, realizing that just as he was a shepherd, now he is the king. But he still wants you to go back and think of the Lord as a shepherd.

What does a shepherd do? A shepherd leads, a shepherd tends, a shepherd feeds, and a shepherd protects. This is who the Lord was to David. The Lord is someone who leads us. We're going to see this in this book. The Lord is someone who takes care of us. He manages us. He tends us. The Lord is someone who feeds us, and the Lord protects us as well.

Jesus went forth doing good and teaching. He said many things about himself. Directly on point He said: *"I am the good shepherd. The good shepherd lays down his life for the sheep. The hired hand is not the shepherd and does not own the sheep. So when he sees the wolf coming, he abandons the sheep and runs away. Then the wolf attacks the flock and scatters it. The man runs away because he is a hired hand* [or a hireling] *and cares nothing for the sheep."* (John 10:11–12 NIV)

A hireling is someone who is just doing a job for the money. The worst thing you can say about any job is, "It's just a job." Find a way to make your job your passion, even if it's the most boring kind of thing. No matter where you work, see yourself as part of the mission. There are a lot of hirelings in every vocation. They just do it for the money. And there are hirelings even in vocational ministry.

But not Jesus. He is the Good Shepherd. What does He do? First, the Good Shepherd sacrifices for the sheep. Aren't you glad for that? Jesus sacrifices for us as His sheep. The greatest example of this, of course, is the cross. He laid down his life for us on the cross, as He gave His life for the sheep. That's what the shepherd does.

David lived centuries before Jesus, so he didn't get to hear about Jesus being a shepherd. We do! The Good Shepherd also owns the sheep. He has a proprietary relationship with us.

Do you see yourself as owned by God or owned by yourself?

There's another verse in the Gospel of John, chapter ten. Jesus said, *"I have other sheep that are not of this sheep pen* [this pasture]." This narrow place. *"I must bring them also."* In other words, "Bring them with me to heaven. They're part of my plan." *"They too will listen to my voice, and there shall be one flock and one shepherd."* (John 10:16 NIV) God has a big flock.

He is talking to a Jewish audience, and he is letting them know that by the time the whole story is done, he is not just going to be the Jewish Messiah; he's going to be the Savior of the whole world. His grace will go out to the Gentiles. There will be a whole other flock out in places like Corinth and Rome and down through time, places like the United States of America. There is going to be one flock following Him—the Good Shepherd.

One day we'll get to heaven. There's a heavenly scene (yet future) that the Apostle John saw in the Book of Revelation, chapter seven. He says, *"They..."* Who? People who have died and gone to heaven. *"They are before the throne of God and serve him day and night in his temple."* Let me pause here. People sometimes ask me, "What are we going to be doing up in heaven forever?" Well, among the things we're going to be doing is we're going to be serving God.

It's not like, "I'll get to do what *I* want to do right now." No, that's not heaven. Heaven will not be like that. You want the best preparation for heaven? Start serving God now, because it will be the norm there. *"And he who sits on the throne* [that's Jesus] *will shelter them with his presence."* Listen to what it says. *"'Never again will they hunger; never again will they thirst. The sun will not beat down on them,' nor any scorching heat."* It goes on. *"For the Lamb..."* Who is the Lamb? It's capitalized. That's Jesus—the Lamb!

"I am the good shepherd." He is the Lamb. How do we know He is the Lamb? Because when He was baptized, John the Baptist saw Him coming and said, *"Behold, the Lamb of God…"* That Jewish audience, they understood sacrificial lamb. They understood the Passover. He is the sacrificial Lamb. He is the Lamb of God, the chosen One of God who will take away the sins of mankind, of the world.

He is still called the Lamb in eternity. That's why we sing songs like "Worthy is the Lamb." He says, *"For the Lamb at the center of the throne will be…"* He is going to be a shepherd, mixing up the metaphor. He is the Lamb, but He is also the shepherd. In other words, the shepherding does not end after life is over on planet earth. *"'He will lead them to springs of living water. And God will wipe away every tear from their eyes.'"*

He is our eternal shepherd. The Lord is not only *a* shepherd, but the Lord is *my* shepherd. This Psalm is packed with personal pronouns. I want you to contrast that for a moment with the Lord's Prayer. *"Our Father which art in heaven, hallowed be thy name. Thy kingdom come… Give us this day our daily bread. […] And lead us not into temptation, but deliver us from evil."*

There is nothing wrong with that. It's a wonderful thing to pray in community for God to bless the community, but here in this Psalm, we find personal pronouns. Now we have already said God has a big flock, so David is not thinking, "I'm not only God's child; I'm his *only* child." There are some Christians who think that. There are some

Christians who think, "I'm not only God's child; I'm his only child. If you're not exactly like me, then you're not of God."

I believe in community. I believe God will raise up people to minister to us during times of trouble. I believe when we're hurting we need friends. But there are times when no one else is around and we don't need anyone but God. We must always be careful not to seek social answers to our spiritual problems.

"The Lord is my shepherd…"

It's not enough for him to be *the* Good Shepherd. It's not enough for him to even be *a* shepherd or *the* Lord. Is he *your* shepherd? Is he *mine*?

Karen and I have been married going on 40 years. We finish each other's sentences. We know what each other is thinking. It's very funny. We know each other very well. Yet, God knows us better than we know ourselves.

The second part of the verse says, *"…I shall not want."*

"The Lord is my shepherd; I shall not want."

These aren't separate; they're interdependent. What does that mean? It doesn't mean you're not going to have problems. It doesn't mean you are not ever going to be hungry. It means you're not going to want for anything.

The Simple Life

You're not going to lack anything. You're going to be able to handle anything.

Adaptability.

"The fear of the Lord leads to life; then one rests content, untouched by trouble." (Psalm 19:23 NIV)

It doesn't say you won't *have* trouble. Did you hear that? It says you won't be *touched* by it. If we're really drawing close to the Lord, the Lord builds protection around us so when we experience even severe trouble, it doesn't do us permanent harm.

We're not touched by it if we understand the role of the Shepherd. Stress is not good for your health, being all torn up all the time, full of envy and conflict.

"…I shall not want."

We can know peace in our current *location*. The grass is not greener on the other side. I love what Erma Bombeck said as a title of one of her books: *"The Grass is Always Greener over the Septic Tank."*

We can know peace with our *property*. Do you have peace about your stuff?

"Keep your lives free from the love of money, and be content with what you have, because God has said, 'Never will I leave you; never will I forsake you. So we say with confidence, 'The Lord is my helper; I will

not be afraid. What can mere mortals do to me?"' (Hebrews 13:5–6 NIV)

We can know peace in spite of our *problems*. Not peace *from* our problems. You're never going to be problem-free. If somebody tells you that, they're lying. You're never going to have peace *from* the storm, but you can have peace *in* the storm.

We can also have peace about our *prospects*. Put the future in the hands of God. We don't know what's out there. We used to sing a song years ago. I can still remember this old couple. I say "old couple." They were probably younger than I am now. They held hands, and they sang this song, a beautiful duet.

> *I don't know about tomorrow.*
> *I just live from day to day.*
> *I don't borrow from its sunshine.*
> *For its skies may turn to gray.*
> *I don't worry o'er the future,*
> *For I know what Jesus said.*
> *And today I'll walk beside him,*
> *For he knows what is ahead.*
> *Many things about tomorrow*
> *I don't seem to understand.*
> *But I know who holds tomorrow,*

The Simple Life

And I know who holds my hand.

– Ira Stanphil
1950

Or to put it another way: *"The Lord is my shepherd; I shall not want."*

Chapter Two
Keys to Personal Revival

I WAS ANSWERING some questions about my writing a while back for someone from the *Huffington Post*. One had to do with how I balance my ministry and my writing, since I write history and fiction. I explained that it was all about the difference between mere *words* and *The Word*.

I love words. I still learn new ones. When we get the *Reader's Digest* (yes—we still subscribe), one of the first things I read is the *Word Power* section. I also love crossword puzzles. And when I'm reading a book, if I come across a word I don't recognize, I'll pull out my phone or go on the computer, and visit Dictionary.com. If I want to remember a particular definition, I'll email it to myself so I have it, because I love words.

I've been a card–carrying dork for decades.

The Simple Life

I remember the first time I heard a particular word. I was five or six years of age. We were at church on a Sunday night. I remember it was dark, and the church building was not well lit. There were some testimonies being shared.

This was before my father became a pastor. He worked at an oil refinery. Sunday night was sometimes the only time he could go to church because of his shift work. There were these two wonderful, elderly men in that church. *Gunning* was their last name. Norman was the shorter one. The taller brother, I can't remember what his name was. They were from Wales. They would sometimes get up and sing duets. I can remember them singing the hymn *"Love Found a Way to Redeem My Soul."* I can still hear their Welsh accent. It was a wonderful thing. They were beloved people. They liked my brother and me and always gave us nickels and candy.

My father later told me that those brothers were saved during the "Welsh Revival." That was the first time I had ever heard the word *revival*. I remember it clearly.

Revival.

The word means many things.

I lived in New York for a dozen years. The most common use of the word *revival* there was of a show coming back to Broadway.

David R. Stokes

It's actually based on a Biblical idea of bringing something back to life that's—to borrow a description from *"The Princess Bride"*—*mostly* dead. Revival is a reawakening.

There have been many great spiritual awakenings in history. But among the most famous and fascinating was the Welsh Revival in 1904. It blazed for about a year through preaching and prayer.

And its impact was felt for decades.

That awakening was a spontaneous thing. There were a couple of key figures, but it was essentially a movement of God. More than 100,000 came to faith in Christ as a result.

One man at the center of it all was a young preacher named Evan Roberts. He later had some difficulties in his life, some emotional issues, but God used him mightily in Wales. Years later, he talked about his experience: "For a long, long time I was much troubled in my soul and my heart by thinking over the failure of Christianity. Oh! it seemed such a failure—such a failure—and I prayed and prayed, but nothing seemed to give me any relief. But one night, after I had been in great distress praying about this, I went to sleep, and at one o'clock in the morning suddenly I was waked up out of my sleep, and I found myself with unspeakable joy and awe in the very presence of the Almighty God."

And for the next year, Roberts and a team of fellow servants conducted meetings all across the region—several each day. Here's a little excerpt from the *South Wales Gazette* in 1904 about the impact of the revival (the war referred to was between Russia and Japan):

"The Revival has been the absorbing theme of thought and discussion. Before it, the War, the state of trade, ordinary and extraordinary political topics, and even football have been thrown into the shade as topics of general conversation. Drunkards have been soberized, publicans have lost much business, conduct on public streets has been elevated, and the police and magistrates have had quieter times. The bottom of the pits have been utilized as centers for prayer and praise meetings, and there has been a general raising of the standard of public life."

It was a monumental spiritual awakening in that coal mining region.

Evan Roberts and company emphasized four simple things. First, confession of all known sin and experiencing forgiveness through Jesus Christ. Second, the removal of anything in the lifestyle about which people felt shame or doubt people . Third, a readiness to obey the Holy Spirit instantly. Fourth, the public profession of the Lord Jesus Christ in baptism.

Not a bad prescription for a personal spiritual reboot.

In the first three verses of this Psalm, there are also principles for such breakthrough moment in our lives.

David R. Stokes

Think back to the year 1989, when the Berlin Wall came down. I actually have a small piece of that infamous symbol of tyranny in my office. The Berlin Wall was the great metaphor for the Cold War, for the fight between Communism and freedom.

President John F. Kennedy visited the wall in 1963 and talked of solidarity with enslaved people when he said, "*Ich bin ein Berliner.*" Then famously two years before the wall came down, President Ronald Reagan said, "Mr. Gorbachev, tear down this wall." These were critical and defining moments, iconic moments during the Cold War, a period that has long fascinated me.

Breakthrough. Can you imagine what it meant to people living in Berlin as that wall was chiseled into oblivion? I realize it hasn't always borne the fruit people wanted it to bear, but that was certainly a game changer. That was certainly a breakthrough moment.

There are such moments in our spiritual lives.

I speak often about my date of salvation: May 12, 1968. That was my ultimate breakthrough moment. I also talk about November 14, 1970. That's when I surrendered to God's call to preach the gospel. Have you had some breakthrough moments in your life? How is your spiritual state? What is your spiritual temperature? Are you on fire for God? Are you lukewarm? Are you cold? Are you indifferent?

The Simple Life

"The Lord is my shepherd; I shall not want. He makes me to lie down in green pastures; He leads me beside the still waters. He restores my soul; He leads me in the paths of righteousness for His name's sake." — Psalm 23:1–3 (NIV)

The Good Shepherd restores us. I want to take that phrase, *"He restores my soul..."* and wrap everything in the verse around it to show you how He does this and why we need this.

Let's be clear. We need this kind of action in our lives because things fade away. Things run down. We go through cycles in our lives. There are moments when we're more spiritually sharp. Please understand, we're all sinners. All of us who are carbon–based life forms are deeply flawed from the start. Sin is our default position. We'd like to think we all make the best choices all the time, but our first instinct or response under pressure tends to be wrong.

We have to counteract that all–too-easy wrong response with a new way—the way of wisdom. A great example is when you're driving in heavy traffic. Somebody cuts you off. I mean, they really seriously cut you off. Do you pull over and say, "Now children in the backseat, this is a person who is in great need. Let's bow our heads and pray for them"? Nope. Usually the horn gets involved. In fact, I lived in the New York City area for a dozen years and I often thought that the only thing that needed to work on my car to pass inspection was the horn.

David R. Stokes

We would all like to think we are basically good people. We'd like to think we don't get mad at certain people. We don't get mad at things. We don't get upset about *this*. We don't get envious of *that*. We don't fear *the other thing*. But sadly, we're all wired the same, and until we've invited God into our lives to fix that wiring, we're prone to sin.

How long we stay in that primal state depends on how we apply the Word to our situation and let the Holy Spirit work in our lives. That's why we need moments of revival. Let me give you a few reasons we need to be restored. I'm looking at the word *restore* as a synonym of *revival*, bringing us back, returning. That's the idea in the Hebrew language.

First, we need to be restored or revived because of *disobedience*. No matter how much Bible we know, we have a tendency, a propensity, toward disobedience to God. King David had access to the throne of God. He had access to spiritual gifts and powers. He had access to opportunities in life, and yet he still made bad choices and disobeyed God.

Sometimes we disobey when God says, "Do *this*," and we don't do it. Sometimes we disobey when God says, "Don't do *this*," and we do it. Disobedience. This is why David prayed in Psalm 51, *"Restore the joy of your salvation and grant me a willing spirit, to sustain me."*

He had lost something.

I believe with all my heart the Bible teaches eternal security. I believe with all my heart the Bible teaches that, the day I got saved, May 12, 1968, I was saved forever. There is nothing I can do that's going to separate me from the love of Christ. There are a lot of compelling reasons to live a good life, but one of them is not a fear of eternal separation from God. I'm saved and secure forever.

I cannot lose my salvation. According to that verse, it's not even mine to lose. *"Restore to me the joy of your salvation…"* That said, there's a lot in life we can lose through sin. There's a lot in life we can lose through disobedience.

I think of a good friend. His testimony is powerful on the subject of loss. Many years ago, he lost everything. He was on the top of his game, one of the most celebrated attorneys in the Commonwealth of Virginia.

Then he lost it all—to alcohol.

He wound up in a sanitarium. While he was there, all of his law partners came and fired him. He was left with nothing. He lost his marriage and family. One day, he walked outside in despair and looked up to the sky and wept and cried, "Lord, help me!"

From that moment on, things began to change for him. God gave him another career. He still holds the record for the largest judgment as an attorney in the history of the Commonwealth of Virginia. He has had a wonderful life, but he knows what it is to lose and to recover.

Not all of us have big swings like that, but I want you to know you can make wrong choices. In fact, everything in your life is about the choices you're making right now. If you make wrong choices, you can lose so much. We need to understand how important it is for us to be obedient. Is God telling you something, teaching you something, directing you to something? Please don't make the deadly mistake of disobedience.

We also need to be restored because we tend to get distracted. We all have a measure of spiritual attention deficit disorder. Did you know that? Not all of us are ADD in some clinically diagnosed way, but all of us have spiritual attention deficit disorder, because this world distracts us.

That's why we're told in First John, chapter two, *"Do not love the world or anything in the world. If anyone loves the world, love for the Father is not in them."* In other words, they can't coexist. *"For everything in the world—the lust of the flesh, the lust of the eyes, and the pride of life—comes not from the Father but from the world. The world and its desires pass away, but whoever does the will of God lives forever."*

The world distracts us. The next thing we know, we're not really focused on the things of God. Are you prone to distraction? I can get very distracted, preoccupied.

Karen and I, a couple of years ago, were having lunch after Sunday services at a restaurant a few miles from our home. I was inside my head throughout my meal, thinking about the services, the sermon, the comments from people. As we paid the bill, it started to rain outside. I had parked a little bit away, so I said, "I'll go get the car. I'll meet you out front. I'll drive around." She said, "Great."

I got in the car and drove home. I was completely lost in thought and forgot my wife!

I was just pulling in the driveway, and the phone rang. The screen said: "Karen." I wondered, "Why is she calling?" It still didn't hit me at that moment. "Hello?" She said, "Um…did you forget something?" Then it hit me like a ton of bricks. I wanted so much to say, "Car trouble. Couldn't start it. Got lost. Forgot where I put it. They stole the car." I drove back.

That trip home was torture by silence. She didn't say a word. I later found out it wasn't really that she was mad. She was spending that time formulating her Facebook status in her head.

Sometimes there is a good reason to be distracted. I remember the day after my mother passed away in December 2002. I flew out to Michigan and rented a car. I made sure it was a big car, because we knew we were going to be hauling people. Family was going to come in. We'd pick up people at the airport. So I got a Lincoln Town Car. That Saturday night, my wife and I, one of my brothers, and my dad went to out to eat.

After the meal, as we were getting ready to leave, I couldn't find the keys to the car. I looked under the table. I looked out in the lobby where we had waited for the table. Finally I walked outside. There in the parking lot was that big car. The door was open, and the engine was running. I had been so preoccupied that I got out of the car and left it that way.

In Detroit.

One time I got out of a car in Akron when I was with my brother-in-law, Ed Holland. Ed and I got out and were walking along. A guy said, "Sir? Sir? Sir?" I said, "What?" "Your car is rolling back." It was on an incline, and I had forgotten to put it in park. It was just rolling down a hill. I ran after it. Ed laughed.

Those moments are humorous, but it's not so funny when we get distracted from the things of God. If you're too busy for the things of God, you're too busy. We get distracted because there's a distance between us and God. There's a disconnect, like Israel when they went into exile. There was a distance, and God had to bring them back.

After the exile, another psalmist wrote, *"When the Lord restored the fortunes of Zion, we were like those who dreamed."* Like a dream come true. "We can't believe we're back. We can't believe we made it back. We made it home," he says. "We were like those who dreamed."

"Our mouths were filled with laughter, our tongues with songs of joy. Then it was said among the nations, 'The Lord has done great things for them.' The Lord has done great things for us, and we are filled with joy. Restore…" There's the word. *"…our fortunes, Lord,*

like streams in the Negev. Those who sow with tears will reap with songs of joy. Those who go out weeping, carrying seed to sow, will return with songs of joy, carrying sheaves with them." (Psalm 126:1–6 NIV)

That's restoration.

How does He restore us? Three things come to mind. First of all, there is the principle of *resting*. I'm not talking about taking a time out *from* God. I'm talking about resting *in* God. *"He makes me to lie down in green pastures."* Again, the shepherd metaphor. David was a shepherd boy. The Middle East, Palestine in particular, is a very arid. There's not a lot of greenery. So it was the shepherd's job to find those places.

"He makes me..." Notice the language. God is compelling this rest. He will make us rest. God looks at us when we have wandered off. The first thing He says is, "You need to stop whatever it is you're doing. You need to lie down in these green pastures. You need to rest."

Sometimes you have to go to a quiet place. Sometimes you have to let anything else and everything else go and focus on your relationship with God.

Just like in counseling people who are married, if there is something wrong in that relationship, it's never going to be fixed, especially if it's a disconnect, unless both parties are willing to make that a priority and take time to do it. I've told men, "You play too much golf. Spend more time with your wife." That's one of the reasons, in my ministry, Mondays have always been my day off. In any place I've pastored, I've always closed the office. I don't do that so guys can have a fun time with guys. I want to see the guys who are on staff spend that day with their families.

Families feeling neglected is one of the great problems in ministry. You go around doing everything for everybody, and those who matter most are neglected. You have to spend some time together. It's the same thing in your spiritual life. If you feel far from God, disconnected from God, God wants you to rest.

He wants you to stop.

I'm sure you have a lot of busy stuff to do, but is there anything as important as your walk with God? Don't you think that if you spend some quality time with God and get yourself restored and rejuvenated and revived, you're going to be better at everything else you're doing? You're going to be more efficient at everything else you're doing?

Not only should we be involved in resting, but also *refueling*. He says, *"He leads me beside the still waters."* Sometimes we need to be replenished. We drink of the water, and we eat of the green grass. This is how God feeds us. The shepherd tends and guides, but he also feeds the flock.

It's interesting. *"He leads me beside the still waters"* is actually something that can be taken a couple of ways. I throw them both out to you because I don't think either is incorrect, because the original Hebrew language is ambiguous on this. I think it gives room, because I do think there are passages that mean one thing, but the Holy Spirit will direct them differently to us in how he applies them.

"He leads me beside the still waters." The most common understanding of that is He finds some still water that's not raging, and He takes me to it so I can drink. That's true. Some translate it *quiet* waters. However, in the Hebrew language, one of the possible renderings in the English language for the word *still* is the word *stagnant* or *putrid*. In other words, there is water that's *still*, but then there's water that's *stagnant*.

When it says, *"He leads me beside the still waters,"* the idea is there are times in your life that the water is not good. He'll lead you *beside* it, not *to* it. He'll lead you literally away from troubled waters in your life. I think they both apply. I think there are times in life where God leads us to this still water and says "Drink!" I think there are also times where we've been drinking bad water, and it's messing with us spiritually. He says, "Get away from this water! It's tainted. It's corrupt," and he takes us to a new and better place for refueling.

He also *redirects* us. He gives me a way to go. He says, *"He leads me in the paths of righteousness for His name's sake."* What does a shepherd do? He leads you. He guides you. Where does he guide you? He doesn't guide you where *you* want to

David R. Stokes

go. The Christian life is not designed to be self-directed. It ought to be God-directed.

When it says, *"He leads me in the paths of righteousness,"* the word *righteousness* is the key. You need to understand what righteousness means—vertically and horizonally.

Vertical righteousness means being right with God, positionally. Horizontal righteousness is learning how to live right on God's terms. He says, *"He leads me in the paths of righteousness..."* It begins with getting "right with God." Are you right with God? Like Evan Roberts preached, is there any un-confessed sin? Anything you are holding onto and won't clean up with God? But then there is the need for practical day-to-day righteousness. God wants us to live righteous lives.

My mother-in-law and her sister traveled to Upstate New York to surprise their older sister on her 85th birthday. They were driving up Route 15 through Pennsylvania. On that route, the big problem is Harrisburg, because you can either go around it, or you can go through it. If you go through it, you have to watch the signs, no matter how many GPS devices you have. So I gave the ladies a big lecture, "You watch the signs. Don't talk. Don't observe." But they got to talking and sure enough got all turned around in Harrisburg.

If you see them, please tell them to phone home.

God wants you to stay on the route. He wants you to be on the safe route, in the right lane, in paths of righteousness. Many times He will have to redirect us because we're going the wrong way. You're convinced you're going the right way. You're convinced you're in the right lane. You're convinced you're going to make it, but you're going the wrong way.

He leads us in paths of righteousness. Why? To give us a better life? That's a benefit, but that's not the reason. He does it for His name's sake. Just step back here for a moment. Did you ever think how much of our modern concept of Christianity is based on the concept of how to get from God what we feel we need? It becomes a theology of self. I believe God meets our needs. I think there's a lot of that here in the Twenty–third Psalm. My shepherd. He does *this* for me. He does *that* for me.

Why does He do it? He does it because He loves us, and certainly He does it for our benefit. He never wants us to forget the ultimate purpose is that His name would be honored. God wants you to live right, not just because you will have a better family, you'll be a better worker, you will be a better citizen. God wants you to live right, because He wants you to be an exhibition before this world of God's name and character.

"The Lord is my shepherd; I shall not want. He makes me to lie down in green pastures; He leads me beside the still waters. He restores my soul; He leads me in the paths of righteousness for His name's sake." (Psalm 23:1–3 NIV)

CHAPTER THREE
No Matter What

YOU WOULD BE hard pressed to find anything more profound, more condensed, in any language or literature than the twenty-third Psalm. David was a shepherd boy who became king. Through the process of inspiration, that mysterious, miraculous dynamic at play that produced ancient ideas that are ever new, God tapped into David's life narrative as a shepherd boy later on in life when he needed it most.

"Though I walk through the valley of the shadow of death, I will fear no evil; for You are with me; Your rod and Your staff, they comfort me." (Psalm 23:4 NIV)

Most commentators and teachers of the Bible believe he wrote this either when he was fleeing during a revolt in the kingdom led by his own son Absalom, or earlier in his life when he was running from the viciousness of King Saul. In that case, he had a comrade, Saul's son Jonathan. They were close friends. There's an interesting passage about that:

"Then David fled from Naioth at Ramah and went to Jonathan and asked, 'What have I done? What is my crime? How have I wronged your father, that he is trying to kill me?' 'Never!' Jonathan replied. 'You are not going to die! Look, my father doesn't do anything, great or small, without letting me know. Why would he hide this from me? It isn't so!'

But David took an oath and said, 'Your father knows very well that I have found favor in your eyes, and he has said to himself, "Jonathan must not know this or he will be grieved." Yet as surely as the Lord lives and as you live, there is only a step between me and death.' Jonathan said to David, 'Whatever you want me to do, I'll do for you.'" (I Samuel 20:14 NIV)

He survived that desperate moment. He made it through. He lived to fight another day—to accomplish mighty deeds for God. But he was acquainted with the idea of impending death. So as the Holy Spirit was processing his youthful shepherding experiences into his later narrative, David ponders mortality:

"Though I walk through the valley of the shadow of death, I will fear no evil; for You are with me; Your rod and Your staff, they comfort me."

This is very powerful. I want you to notice something interesting about the language in the Psalm. I've written a couple of screenplays based on a few of my books. One of

David R. Stokes

the things you have to learn when writing a screenplay is about the point of view—POV. I want you to think about David and his point of view in this. David is talking to *himself*.

Do you talk to yourself? Do you ever yell at yourself? Do you talk back? Thoughts just come and you sort of have to shout them back down? That's what was going on as David developed this precious Psalm. In fact, any emotion you will ever experience you'll find in the book of Psalms: depression, joy, peace, safety, fear, and anger. You name it; it's there.

In the forty–second Psalm, a severely depressed man asked himself, *"Why are you cast down, O my soul?"* He was talking to himself. Some of this self–talk is affirmation. That's the way it is in the first part of Psalm twenty–three. David was reflecting. He was concerned—maybe even fearful—about his life. He was in a dangerous spot. He had some big problems. And maybe just then he saw some sheep in the distance, and the scene reminded him of back in the day when he was a shepherd. God used that. God will use your life narrative to remind you about his power.

It is at this point in the writing of this Psalm that something powerful, but subtle happens. As David thinks about his own mortality, he stops talking *about* the Lord and starts talking *to* the Lord.

"For you are with me; your rod and your staff they comfort me."

The Simple Life

There are two things we are supposed to be doing in this world if we love God. We should talk *about* God and talk *to* God. They're both important.

"The valley of the shadow of death..."

Don't think of this as a big long valley with a babbling brook and pretty flowers. Think of a rugged ravine, like where the Good Samaritan found the man dying on the road in Luke, chapter ten. A place where criminals hide, and where the shadows play scary tricks on the eyes and mind.

It takes two things to make a shadow: *substance* and *light*.

When you're in a rough place and problems grow large and seem to threaten, it is time to pray. It is time to not just talk *about* God, but *to* God.

As you read the Psalms, you'll notice something revealing. In one verse or two verses, the writer will be testifying. Then, other times he'll just be talking to God. It's seamless. I think that's how God wants our internal conversation to run. Thoughts come into our mind. We praise God for something. Somebody is next to us. We tell them something God did. Then we talk to God.

That's what it means to pray without ceasing. It's not a ritualistic kind of thing. It's a spiritual breathing process. He says, *"Though I walk through the valley of the shadow of death..."* He's familiar with valleys, because he had to take the sheep there. *"I will fear no evil. You're with me. Your rod and your staff comfort me."*

Let's talk about this idea of the shadow of death a little bit. What does this mean? Well, it means death, yes, but the key word is *shadow*. It's representative. It's an exaggeration. It's a phantasm. It's something that lurks, something we can't quite make out, but it scares us. The light hits something the wrong way, and a shadow haunts us.

We live in a world where there's a culture of death. People are fascinated with death. My oldest daughter has two teenagers. They love to watch the show *The Walking Dead*. It's about zombies. My grandson asked, "Grandpa, don't you like zombies?" I said, "I've been in ministry for 38 years. I've preached to them Sunday after Sunday. They're looking at you, and sometimes they grunt and you don't know if they're going to bite you or if what they have is contagious. No, don't need that. I mean, give me *Tom and Jerry*, *Huckleberry Hound*, you know, stuff like that." But we have a culture of death, and it's a pretty serious problem. We're preoccupied with it. We are never far from the shadow of death.

We've all experienced personal loss and grief. We carry a burden of sorrow because we're missing someone. We're surrounded by what David called the "shadow of death."

A while back, I was called to a local hospital on a rainy night. A friend of mine was in the emergency room. He had a stroke—at 38 years of age. He didn't see it coming.

Pretty serious stuff. They found out he needed surgery on his heart. There was a small hole—it had been there all of his life. The surgery was successful and he is back to his life.

"The valley of the shadow of death…"

The shadow of death. It's a valley, something we must go *through*. We get through it because we have the promise of ultimate victory. *"The end will come,"* Paul told the Corinthians, *"when he hands over the kingdom to God the Father after he has destroyed all dominion, authority, and power."* (I Corinthians 15:24 NIV)

The Bible says He must reign until He has put all enemies under His feet. The last enemy to be destroyed is death. I don't know how many times I've been in situations at gravesides through these years, and invariably I am drawn to these powerful words:

"Behold, I show you a mystery; we shall not all sleep, but we shall all be changed, in a moment, in the twinkling of an eye, at the last trump: for the trumpet shall sound…and we shall be changed. For this corruptible must put on incorruption, and this mortal must put on immortality…then shall be brought to pass the saying that is written, death is swallowed up in victory.

O death, where is thy sting? O grave, where is thy victory? The sting of death is sin; and the strength of sin is the law. But thanks be to God, [who gives] *us the victory through our Lord Jesus Christ."* (I Corinthians 15:51–57 KJV)

No matter what we walk through—He is with us. We would like to think the valley of the shadow of death is when we wander away. Wrong. *"He leads me in paths of righteousness, even when He leads me through the valley of the shadow of death."* He doesn't lead us *to* the valley. He leads us *through* the valley.

We tend to want God to find us a "work–around" when we face painful things. We're always wanting God to build a bypass around something we don't want to experience. But God has never promised us that. I'd rather be by a green pasture than in a scary ravine where there are ominous shadows, but I can't avoid those moments in life.

So how do you overcome the fear?

What is fear? There's a good fear. There's a lot in the Bible about fearing God. There's a good kind of fear that keeps you from doing stuff to damage yourself or others. But most everyday fear is rooted in the Greek word, *phobos*, from which we get our word *phobia*. When we think of fear in a negative sense, that primal emotion, it's very paralyzing. It immobilizes us and sometimes even tortures us.

"Fear hath torment…" (I John 4:18 KJV)

I like this acrostic for fear: **F**alse **E**xpectations **A**ppearing **R**eal.

Bishop T.D. Jakes says: "Resist your fear. Fear will never lead you to a positive end. Go for your faith and what you believe."

The Simple Life

The twenty–third Psalm gives three key thoughts.

"You are with me. Your rod and Your staff, they comfort me."

This speaks of three things absolutely essential for the conquest of fear.

1. *God's presence.* "You are with me." One of my favorite words in all of the English language and in the entire Bible is that simple little connector, that little word *with*. Think of that. That word says so much. It makes all the difference in the world.

My youngest grandson, Sawyer, is a wonderful kid. He is a very, very effervescent kind of little boy. When he was about a year and a half, just a few months after he started to walk, he slipped away for just a couple of minutes—like kids tend to do. He wandered all the way downstairs, and opened a door and walked out into the garage. I think a light probably came on at the time the door opened, but then the door automatically closed behind him, and a moment later the light went off.

He started to scream and cry. To freak out.

But no one could hear him. Finally, after a few minutes—not a terribly long time, but it probably seemed like hours to Sawyer—they found him.

Today, Sawyer has no memory of that event—but yet he does. There's something interesting about Sawyer. We are "full service" grandparents. We get to see our grandkids so much, that we are thinking of just asking their parents when *they* want to see them. When Sawyer is over, if you leave the room, he will follow you to the other room. He loves to watch football. He doesn't care whether it's football from now or a replay of a bowl game from 1992—he loves it. I'll turn on a college game from two and a half years ago, and he'll be focused on the screen. He'll just sit there and watch it. "Watch it with me, Grandpa," he'll say. So I do—for a short time. But when I have to go into the other room for something, he follows me. Why?

Because he wants to be *with* somebody.

It's going to be cool when Sawyer gets married. His wife is never going to have a moment by herself ever, ever, ever, because he's going to want to be with her.

His sense of security is all wrapped up in a four-letter word: *with*.

When you are fearful, surround yourself with the presence of God. Let His presence become more powerful to you than the presence of that shadow that may look like death.

2. *God's protection.* He protects us. Are the "rod" and the "staff" the same thing or are they two different things? In the Hebrew language, it is clear they reference two different things. However, it is true that in some cases there are shepherds who have combined both functions into one, but likely during David's time the rod was like a club and

The Simple Life

shorter than a staff. The staff was the long stick you think of with the crook on the end. The purpose of the club was not to beat the sheep. Shepherds didn't beat the sheep. The purpose of the club was to ward off enemies, like the wolves, or to knock something down to prepare the way. It was designed as a tool for protection.

3. *God's pressure*. That's the staff. It has the crook at the end. Why the crook? Well, if the sheep get out of line, he's able to go over and gently put that around a neck and bring it back to the flock. It's used for discipline. There's some pain. I mean, you get a crook around your neck and it's probably going to hurt a little bit, but it's better than wandering off a cliff.

Sometimes, in order to get us to think straight, God will deliberately allow us to go through pain, because it's the only way we can learn. The staff is about discipline. Like we discipline our children. We do it in love. We do it gently.

Some days are better than others, and you may wonder, "Why am I going through this?" Because God is allowing you to go through this. You didn't wander into the valley of the shadow of death. He's there with you. See, on the other side of that valley with all of these ugly shadows there's some calm water. There's some green grass. There's a blessing over there.

You must face your fear.

Think about death. Death is separation. So this doesn't just define physical death. How about the death of a dream? How about the death of a relationship? How about the death of a phase in your life? Maybe you get the empty nest, or you're going from singleness to marriage, and there's a disconnect. How about when you uproot and move to another place? You have to make all kinds of new friends.

There are a lot of ways disconnect comes into our lives and causes pain, and we'd rather not go through it. But God is there, and his rod will protect us from the problems, and his staff will gently discipline us. That's the message—no matter what, no matter where, no matter when, no matter how, no matter why.

Did you notice how the verse ends? *"Your rod and Your staff, they comfort me."* You wouldn't think a shepherd's crook around the neck would be comforting. He didn't mean that the crook itself was comforting, but the fact God cares enough to know, to watch, to guide, and to be with me, provides me comfort. It doesn't take the problem away. It doesn't take the pain away, but it helps me manage it for His honor and His glory.

"[Even] though I walk through the valley of the shadow of death, I will fear no evil; for You are with me; Your rod and Your staff, they comfort me."

Chapter Four
A Table in the Wilderness

GOD HAS CALLED us to experience a measure of simplicity and rest in the midst of challenge and complexity. He doesn't want us to be *overwhelmed* by life and the world; he wants us to *overcome* it. The way we overcome it is by having the capacity to process life in compliance with His Word and respond to it accordingly.

"The Lord is my shepherd; I shall not want. He makes me lie down in green pastures. He leads me beside still waters. He restores my soul. He leads me in paths of righteousness for his name's sake. Even though I walk through the valley of the shadow of death, I will fear no evil, for you are with me; your rod and your staff, they comfort me. You prepare a table before me in the presence of my enemies; you anoint my head with oil; my cup overflows. Surely goodness and mercy shall follow me all the days of my life, and I shall dwell in the house of the Lord forever."

The Simple Life

This is an all—encompassing creed for anyone who longs for a relationship with God on a personal level.

"You prepare a table before me in the presence of my enemies; you anoint my head with oil; my cup overflows."

Let's look at three concepts.

1. *Fellowship*. I was born and raised Baptist—not just Baptist, but Fundamental, Independent, Baptist. That's like Baptist on steroids. I interviewed Governor Mike Huckabee a few years ago. We talked about our common backgrounds. I play the bass guitar. He plays the bass guitar. We talked about growing up Baptist.

He told me a story about how when he was a kid in elementary school in Arkansas they had religion day in their school, and they said, "Everybody, bring in a symbol of your religion." One of his Jewish friends brought in a menorah. A Catholic girl in the class brought in a crucifix. He, being a Baptist, brought in a covered dish.

In fact, the word *fellowship* provokes a Pavlovian response in some church people—they smell food and start to salivate. "Let's have some fellowship" is often church-speak for sharing a meal. But the Greek word for fellowship is from the word *koinonia*, which means a sharing in common. It is also a root of the word, *community*. And it can also mean, *partnership*.

David R. Stokes

It's something much more in depth, and it involves a cluster of common things we share. When you find in the New Testament they're talking about fellowship, the church in fellowship and fellowship with God, it's talking about much more than just a social or superficial kind of relationship.

"You prepare a table before me in the presence of my enemies."

Let me give you a couple of terms: *relationship* and *fellowship*. My father lives in Florida. He is in his eighties. When you're in eighties, you have to move to Florida. I think it's a law. I'm his oldest son. That's a genetic fact. I have a relationship with my dad that no matter if either one of us wanted to change it (which we don't), we can't. If you've ever been around my dad and around me, you know there are some mannerisms I get from him. We have that relationship. I am born of his seed.

Fellowship with my dad is based on that relationship, but it's also conditional. For instance, when I was growing up, if my father told me to do something and I didn't do it, our relationship would be the same, but our "fellowship" in such moments could be strained. Fellowship has to do with the give and take in a relationship.

Karen and I have been married since May 28, 1976. We have a marriage license someplace. People came to our wedding. We have pictures to prove it. That's our *relationship*. But our *fellowship* is based on how it is going day-to-day. Sometimes we have great fellowship. Sometimes we disagree. Sometimes we may be at odds with each other for a short period of time, we have a disagreement, and the fellowship is somewhat strained.

I want you to think of that as a picture of spiritual living, because just as my relationship with my dad is a genetic fact, so my relationship with God is based on a genetic fact. I am Gerald Stokes' son because I was born of his seed. I am God's son because I was born again. The Bible says, *"...not of corruptible seed, but of incorruptible, by the Word of God, which lives and abides forever."* I have an undeniable relationship with him.

But the intimacy we have with God ebbs and flows. There are times when we get so distracted and so preoccupied with other aspects of life that we're not as close to the Lord as we ought to be, and everything becomes foggy and unclear. We have a coldness that's in our heart instead of the fire and the joy of the Lord. What's going on there is not that our relationship has changed, but our fellowship is not as it should be. You can apply that principle to friendships and other relationships. I want you to think of fellowship as something more *subjective* and relationship as *objective*.

What I'm saying in this point is that God is always doing things to remind us that we have a relationship with Him, and he calls us to have fellowship with Him. He wants us to be close to him. He has provided all these open doors for us to have this wonderful, vibrant relationship with Him.

David R. Stokes

But like any relationship, it depends upon communication. Communion and communication are similar terms. They're based on the same idea. Fellowship is not only having a social relationship with people, but fellowship is also vertical. It's having a close relationship with God. I'm here to tell you that I have had an actual spiritually genetic relationship based on being born again since May 12, 1968, when I opened my heart to Christ. That has never changed. That's always been secure. It's sealed in heaven.

But there have been times in my life when my fellowship with God has been strained, not because He has changed anything but because I've allowed myself to drift from him or I've allowed things to come between me and God. When it says, *"You prepare a table before me in the presence of my enemies,"* He is calling us to this kind of fellowship. He is saying, "Come back."

He talks about enemies. We don't like to think about enemies, but we've all had them. We're to love our enemies and pray for those who spitefully use us. An enemy is something or someone contrary.

We all deal with contrary forces in life. You may even have people working against you, but always remember that God delights in blessing us with a bountiful table in their sight.

Psalm 78 is from Asaph. It's a *maskil*, which is a didactic kind of poetic psalm. It talks about the history of the ancient children of Israel. They came out from Egypt in the great exodus. The Red Sea parted. God did so many miracles, and yet the people forgot they had been delivered from slavery. They began to question God. They drifted into unbelief, cynicism, negativity, and a critical spirit.

It says, *"But they continued to sin against him, rebelling in the wilderness against the Most High. They willfully put God to the test by demanding the food they craved. They spoke against God; they said, 'Can God really spread a table in the wilderness?'"* In other words, "He has brought us out here in the middle of nowhere. Is God really going to provide a banquet for us out here?"

"True, he struck the rock, and water gushed out, streams flowed abundantly, but can he also give us bread?" "Water is one thing. It came out of a rock." That ought to be a sign. "But what about bread?" *"'Can he supply meat for his people?' When the Lord heard them, he was furious; his fire broke out against Jacob, and his wrath rose against Israel, for they did not believe in God or trust in his deliverance."* (Psalm 78:17–22 NIV)

It's easy to be hard on the ancient Israelites and say, "What a bunch of knuckleheads!" Yet, we are prone to repeat their history. We forget about what God has provided for us. We're in the wilderness of life. All of life is a wilderness. There's a lot of wandering, a lot of aimlessness. God has provided this table for us, and sometimes we get to be like those people: *"Can God really provide a table for us in the wilderness? Sure, he gave us water, but can he give us bread?"*

God did. Manna from heaven. Eventually He sent meat. God is always providing what His people need. He provides the Bread of Life, Jesus Christ, to us for salvation. The simple life always involves the idea of having a fundamental relationship with God through Christ and then keeping that relationship fresh.

When Karen and I were dating, I'd open her door and let her in the car. In those days, we had bench seats. It was a cool time to date. I had a 1971 lime green LTD. What a hot car. She got in, and she was sitting over against the passenger door. I said, "You can move a little closer if you want to."

Sadly, she didn't want to, not on that date—which makes me wonder why I'm mentioning it now.

I have to admit, I don't always open my wife's door now. Every once in a while, we'll pull up some place or at home, and I'll get out of the car, and maybe I'll go check the mail in the mailbox in front of the house. The garage door is already open. I start to walk past the car. She is still sitting in her seat looking straight. Then, because I'm not always clueless, I realize what's happening. She is being subtle. There have been times I've actually gone into the house. Where's Karen? She is still sitting in the car. I go back out. "I'm sorry, dear." I let her out, and we go into the house— the cold, cold house.

2. *Empowerment.* I see that in this verse. *"You prepare a table before me in the presence of my enemies; you anoint my head with oil."* That's empowerment. Anointing spoke of many things. It was an unguent for healing. You see that in the book of James.

Anointing can also be about empowerment. For instance, when Samuel the prophet went to Jesse's house in Bethlehem looking for the future king, and David the shepherd boy was chosen. Samuel anointed him with oil. That was a sanctifying and empowering act. It was symbolic.

The Bible uses the term *anointing* in many, many ways. In the book of 1 John, it tells all believers that we already have an internal anointing from God. We've already been set apart by God for his service. I want to use it as a term of empowerment how God anoints and God wants to empower us.

I think of boldness. I think of our willingness to take a stand for Christ. The mark of the early church was boldness that was wrought by the Spirit of God. They were willing to take a stand. Paul echoed that when he told the Romans, *"For I am not ashamed of the gospel of Christ: for it is the power of God unto salvation to every one that believes; to the Jew first, and also to the Greek."* (Romans 1:16 NIV)

When God empowers us, He wants us to understand that we are a special people. We have His mark. We have His presence in our lives. I want you to think about how God empowers us. There is a difference between empowerment and entitlement.

God wants all of us to do different things as part of his bigger plan. We're not clones. It's not a cookie–cutter kind of thing. God called me to be doing what I'm doing now.

David R. Stokes

God calls other people to different aspects of life and ministry. In other words, whatever God commands you to do, whatever God directs you to do, whatever God calls you to do, he will provide you the strength you need. He will do it. It says in 1 Thessalonians, chapter five, *"Faithful is he that calls you, who also will do it."*

Another way to say it is that God's callings imply God's enabling. In other words, technically speaking, when God puts something before you and it's clear He wants you to do this, the answer should never be, "I can't," because implicit in what He is asking you to do, is the reality that He is going to provide the strength for you to do it. The answer may be because we're weak, "I won't," because it's difficult or challenging, but if God asks you to do it, calls you to do it, you can't say, "I can't," because God will give you what you need.

Sometimes natural ability can get in the way of God's empowerment. Listen to what it says in Psalm 92:

"It is good to give thanks to the Lord, to sing praises to the Most High. It is good to proclaim your unfailing love in the morning, your faithfulness in the evening, accompanied by the ten-stringed harp and the melody of the lyre. You thrill me, Lord, with all you have done for me! I sing for joy because of what you have done. O Lord, what great works you do! And how deep are your thoughts. Only a simpleton would not know, and only a fool would not understand this: though the wicked sprout like weeds and evildoers flourish, they will be destroyed forever. But you, O Lord, will be exalted forever. Your

enemies, Lord, will surely perish; all evildoers will be scattered. But you have made me as strong as a wild ox. You have anointed me with the finest oil."

That's empowerment. Yes, sometimes we feel under equipped and underprepared, but the very fact that you have trial and trouble should be a reminder that God believes in us because He will never give us anything we can't handle.

3. *Passion.* Be passionate about something you're doing. It doesn't mean you have to be like a cheerleader and over the top, but make sure your, *"cup overflows."* Years ago, in 1980, I was involved with my father–in–law in planting a church in Canarsie, Brooklyn, New York. We would go out, and we'd try to get people to come to our fledgling storefront church. We'd knock on doors. In Brooklyn. That's a tough place.

Like banging your head against a brick wall, tough.

There was this coffee shop. They hadn't heard of Starbucks or Dunkin' Donuts. All the waitresses were armed and dangerous. This was the real New York kind of place—a dive coffee shop. This was long before Brooklyn became cool and trendy.

All the cups had saucers underneath them. The lady would come over. "Whaddaya want, honey? She'd pour the coffee, and she'd always pour it sloppily so it would just flop over onto the saucer. I love coffee. I mean, I *love* coffee. I spill

David R. Stokes

two or three cups a day. I drink a lot more than that. Many days, I start with a Venti Red Eye from Starbucks. That's a big and bold coffee with a shot of espresso in it. That will *really* get you going.

So I couldn't stand to see that coffee in that saucer. I didn't take a napkin. No, no, no, no, no. I'd make sure to drink every last drop. My cup overflowed. Do you ever think about my joy overflows? My cup *overflows*. *"My cup runneth over"* is the way it reads in the classic King James Version.

Joy. Passion. Do you know when we really make a difference in the lives of others? When our lives overflow. The real supernatural stuff that changes lives and helps people happens on the overflow. The problem with most of us is we're only living half-empty.

Are you full enough of the Holy Spirit? Are you full enough of the Lord? Does the Lord have enough of you? You really minister on the overflow. I'm an extemporaneous speaker, which doesn't mean impromptu. Usually if you're an extemporaneous speaker, you have to prepare more than if somebody wrote down every word and said it, because you preach from the overflow.

You minister from the overflow. You witness from the overflow. You want to share your faith? Be an overflowing kind of person. Have some passion about it. When something happens and God does something in your life, does your cup overflow? Peter said, *"Beloved, do not think it strange concerning the fiery trial which is to try you, as though some strange thing happened to you; but rejoice to the extent that you partake of Christ's sufferings, that…"*

What? Partake of Christ's sufferings? In other words, Jesus died. He suffered. You're going to suffer, too. That's not bad news. That is the amazing thing. Rejoice! *"…that when His glory is revealed, you may also be glad with exceeding joy."* Overflowing joy. Fellowship, empowerment, and passion: theses are vital keys to the simple life.

When our church observes communion, we take a little piece of bread and a small cup of the fruit of the vine to symbolize the broken body and the shed blood of Christ. It's about remembering Christ's death until He returns.

Clean, clear, close—three words that make all the difference. Life is better when we are clean before God. Your life is better when we are close to God. That is when life becomes more clear—things make sense. There's a direct relationship between intimacy, purity, and clarity. If you want to see more of God working in your life, look at those two other things: intimacy and purity in life.

The Twenty–third Psalm is part of a triad in the book of Psalms (chapters 22, 23, 24). They're known as Messianic Psalms. The Twenty–third Psalm is obvious. He is a loving shepherd (God is). If you read Psalm 24, it's all about imagery about a coming King. It's futuristic. It's about the Messiah as the King of Kings and the Lord of Lords. The Twenty–third Psalm is about Him while he was on the earth saying, *"I am the good shepherd."*

David R. Stokes

If you read Psalm 22, this is where something Jesus uttered on the cross comes from. *"My God, my God, why hast thou forsaken me?"* The Twenty-second psalm is about a dying Savior. You have a dying Savior, you have a loving Shepherd, and you have a coming King.

In Psalm 22, it says, "They pierced my hands and my feet." It talks about bones not being broken, but put out of joint. It's a description of what would eventually be known as crucifixion, even though such a painful way to die had not been thought of yet. It would come later out of many cultures, but it's the Romans who perfected it in all it's horror.

The purpose of crucifixion was to provide the most public, humiliating, brutal deterrent to crime (or what they deemed as crime) possible. It was designed to be brutal. It was designed to be humiliating. It was designed to prolong the agony. It was designed to be public. It was a public execution.

It begs the question… *Why would God in his foreknowledge* (writing before it) *co-opt that?* Now when we see the image of the cross, we're filled with wonder. It's about redemption. It's about love. It's about all of this.

But, crucifixion itself is a great picture of redemption.

Think of it this way. If God can take something as brutal and barbaric, as awful and humiliating and torturous as the rite of crucifixion (a common form of capital punishment in that world) and turn it into, by virtue of what Jesus suffered there, the ultimate symbol of hope and love and mercy, then there's not a mess we can make have that he can't turn into something positive. That's ultimate redemption.

When He was crucified that day, I think that's part of what He was telling us. "I'm willing to go through this for you, and you can handle anything. If I can turn this ugliness around into something beautiful and joyful that you even sing about today, then what can you do with anything that's painful or hurtful in your life?"

A few weeks before he died in November 1963, President John F. Kennedy went out to Arlington to lay a wreath at the Tomb of the Unknown Soldier on Veterans Day. He lingered a bit, and he found himself on a little slope not far from Robert E. Lee's home, which is on the grounds. It was a beautiful fall day with the foliage in full color. He remarked to somebody nearby he thought that was the most beautiful place on earth.

A few weeks later, of course, he traveled to Dallas. That day, that had just changed from rain to brightness and unseasonable warmth, suddenly turned tragic. As the slain President's closest friends were preparing to take the body back to Washington, DC, Clint Hill, the man who climbed on the back of the limo to push Mrs. Kennedy back into her seat after the final shot, asked Jackie if wanted to change her clothes. She was wearing that now iconic pink suit. It was covered in blood. Her answer was, "No, I want them to see what they've done to him." I always wondered what she meant by that (who were "they"?), but I think we understand the meaning. Somebody did something to the man she loved, and she wanted that to be seen.

The human story is a story of bloodshed from the days of Cain and Abel and that blood crying out from the ground. The blood is essential. Leviticus 17:11 says, *"For the life of the flesh is in the blood: and I have given it to you upon the altar to make an atonement for your souls: for it is the blood that makes an atonement for the soul."*

We think of the shedding of blood as something awful. But it had to be that way. In hindsight, we know that. When Jesus came to be baptized, John the Baptist said, *"Behold! The Lamb of God who takes away the sin of the world!"* It was a Jewish audience. They understood the "lamb" metaphor. They were people who observed the Passover and the Passover lamb and the very sacrificial system. Jesus had come to be the ultimate sacrificial lamb. He shed his blood, and He gave up the ghost when he cried, *"It is finished."* Paul says we are bought with a price. Therefore, glorify God in your body and spirit, which belong to God. That price was the blood of Christ.

This table in the wilderness, that the children of Israel mocked, looks forward to a time in the future when he is going to be the coming King. We live in the wilderness between Calvary and the kingdom, between the cross and heaven.

CHAPTER FIVE
Now is Forever

LIFE CAN BE very complex, but the great answers to life, I am convinced (certainly the *biblical* answers), are simple. They're not always easy, but they are simple.

There are concepts that are simple enough for a child to grasp. Jesus said, "Except you become as a child…" We talk about the nature of faith. We often will say it's childlike faith. It is a simple, trusting faith. For example, there used to be a tract that was handed out in tract evangelism called "God's Simple Plan of Salvation."

This simplicity can be a problem. To paraphrase Paul's challenge to the Corinthians, "I really fear for you people, because just as the Serpent in the Garden of Eden deceived (or *beguiled* is the word that's used) Eve, so you might be deceived because of the *simplicity* that is in the gospel."

The Simple Life

In other words, when you hear that salvation is by grace through faith plus nothing, it's counterintuitive to everything we know about religion. Grace is unmerited favor. You can't earn it. You can't purchase it. It's already been purchased for us through the blood of Christ. It's so simple some people stumble over it, and there has to be more to it. There's another shoe that has to drop. There has to be more to the puzzle.

The Twenty-third Psalm is a common go-to passage during times of difficulty. We may think we know it, but it is a mine whose wealth will constantly amaze us.

"Surely goodness and mercy shall follow me all the days of my life..."

Every time I hear that term *surely goodness*, I think about when I was a young boy... I must have been four or five years of age (before my dad was a pastor). My pastor's name was Kennedy. The same with my President. It was a little confusing at times.

The church had a ladies' trio. One of the songs they'd sing was a popular song back in the 50s and the 60s, and it was based on this phrase, *"Surely goodness and mercy shall follow me all the days of my life..."* I had in my head that "Shirley Goodness" was one of the lady's names. So I would say, "Dad, when is Shirley Goodness going to sing again?"

"Surely goodness and mercy shall follow me all the days of my life..."

David R. Stokes

The simple life is a *godly* life. I don't think there's any disputing that we ought to try to live good lives. Good works do not save us, but they have their place. They are not the root of salvation, but they are the fruit of salvation. They are not the cause of salvation, but they are to be the effect of salvation. You can't work your way into heaven.

This is what the Scriptures say. We should be pursuing goodness, as we're going to talk about in this point. Here's what he says. He says, "What you need to know is that goodness and mercy follow you if you're a child of God."

In fact, when Jesus talks about the Holy Spirit in his Gospels (in John's gospel particularly), he uses a word that comes across to us in the English the *comforter*. He would say, "The Comforter is going to come." That's a reference to the Holy Spirit. The word *comforter* comes from the Greek word *parakletos*, which means one who is called alongside to help.

Because the Holy Spirit has been called alongside, I can overcome fear. And he is not only with me, but he makes sure that what follows after me is awesome—goodness and mercy.

The word *follow* in the Hebrew language is a very aggressive term—like pursuing something with passion. It indicates that we are almost harassed in a godly way by goodness and mercy.

You may not always feel this goodness. You may think, "I could go for some mercy. I could go for some goodness right now in my life." But it's there. It's shadowing you. It's not death that's shadowing you; it's all the good things of life.

"…all the days of my life…"

He is following me, so I should be living a godly life, the simple life. One of the ways we avoid complicating our lives is by living simply according to his commands. It's when we stray that we find life much more difficult.

In the New Testament book of First Timothy, Paul told a young preacher, *"Have nothing to do with godless myths and old wives' tales; rather, train yourself to be godly. For physical training is of some value, but godliness has value for all things, holding promise for both the present life and the life to come."* (I Timothy 4:7–8 NIV)

This is exactly what he is talking about in Psalm 23:6.

"Surely goodness and mercy shall follow me all the days of my life…"

We see what godliness means as we see some other elements added. Peter talks about the *"…divine power* [of God] *has given us everything we need for a godly life…"* If you're saved, you don't need anything more from God. He has already given it to you. It's a matter of tapping in and discovering it.

"...everything we need for a godly life through our knowledge of him who called us by his own glory and goodness." God is good. *"Through these he has given us his very great and precious promises..."* That's what the Twenty-third Psalm is filled with. *"...so that through them..."* The promises. By affirming these things, and remembering these things and applying them in the right way, we grow into the kind of people God wants us to be.

"...you may participate in the divine nature [supernatural nature], *having escaped the corruption in the world caused by evil desires. For this very reason, make every effort..."* So work hard at this, in other words. *"...to add to your faith goodness; and to goodness, knowledge; and to knowledge, self-control; and to self-control, perseverance; and to perseverance, godliness, and to godliness, mutual affection; and to mutual affection, love."* (II Peter 1:3-7 NIV)

This is the life to which God has called us. The answers may not be easy, but they are usually simple. It's not for the theological elite, not for people who can understand the esoteric and the mysterious. It's for all of us. It's common to us. It is His grace. It is His mercy. He wants us to be able to discern these things and to apply them to our lives.

Goodness and mercy are following me all the days of my life. I may not always feel like that, but God's goodness is there. It's with me, it's in me, and it's pursuing me. It is my default position. It is what's behind me. It has my back. This is what God is saying.

The Simple Life

The second thing about goodness and mercy (and it's directly on point for the concept of the title of this chapter: *Now is Forever*) is that the simple life is also eternal life right *now*.

"And I will dwell in the house of the Lord for ever."

Now if I were writing that, I might not say, *"...AND I will dwell in the house of the Lord for ever."* I'd say: *"...THEN I'll dwell in the house..."* I'd put *then*, because we look at life as *now* and *then*. I'm here *now*, but *then* I'm going to be up there.

But that's not how eternity works. Eternity is different than time. We are all time travelers. We are all traveling eternally through time. Eternity doesn't mean to exist forever. Eternity is different than that.

I was conceived in October of 1955. Life begins at conception. That is my biological belief. People say, "You shouldn't push your theological belief on the public about pro–life." Well, pro–life is not my *theological* belief. My theological belief is not that life begins at *conception*. That's my *biological* belief. My theological belief is life begins *before* conception.

God knew me before the foundation of the world. That's when I began. The great story of whatever has happened began then. Then May 12, 1968, I received Christ, and I tapped into that power. I'm going to live forever.

David R. Stokes

"And so shall we ever be with the Lord." (I Thessalonians 4:17 NIV)

Eternal life doesn't mean existence from now on. Eternal life means life that never had a beginning and never has an end. It's not me. Eternal life is the life of *God*. Eternal life is the life of the Eternal One. That's why Moses, when he said, "Who shall I say is sending me to Pharaoh?" "Say that I Am." Jesus said, *"before Abraham was, I am."* (John 8:58 NIV)

The eternal *now*.

God never had a beginning. God never will have an end. I had a beginning. I was thought of, I was known, I was foreknown, I had a beginning. You had a beginning. What does it mean for me to receive eternal life? It means that one day I tied my story to God's story by receiving him by faith. Think of a supernatural power line that never begins and never ends. And then think about my line connected with that line at one point—and from that point on.

Eternal life is not my existence forever. The eternal life is the life of the Eternal One. It means I've received Christ. That's what the Bible teaches. I'm in eternity right now. It's like space. People say, "Oh, I'd love to go to outer space." This planet is moving through space right now. We're already there. We may not think of it because of atmosphere and various limitations.

It's not a matter of, "Surely goodness and mercy shall follow you all the days of your life. *Then* when you die you will dwell in the house of the Lord." That's not how David saw it. He saw it as seamless. "Take one step. Take another step." The next step is after death. He says *and*—not *then*.

"...and I will dwell in the house of the Lord for ever."

In fact, David saw his spiritual existence as involving the house of the Lord right now. Listen to what he says in Psalm 27. *"One thing I ask from the Lord, this only do I seek: that I may dwell in the house of the Lord all the days of my life, to gaze on the beauty of the Lord and to seek him in his temple. For in the day of trouble..."*

There's no trouble in heaven. This is about earth!

"For in the day of trouble he will keep me safe in his dwelling; he will hide me in the shelter of his sacred tent and set me high upon a rock. Then my head will be exalted above the enemies who surround me; at his sacred tent I will sacrifice with shouts of joy; I will sing and make music to the Lord." (Psalm 27:4–6 NIV)

What is the house of the Lord? It's a term that's used very generically in Scripture. It's a concept that means a place to meet with God. Like David once said, *"I was glad when they said unto me, 'Let us go into the house of the Lord.'"* It was also a place that had an altar. We find that concept in the days of Jacob and Abraham.

David R. Stokes

It is where God is. What does it mean to us? Well, we don't have a temple where we go meet God. The Bible says, *"In the beginning was the Word..."* Word. Logos. It's another name for Jesus. *"In the beginning was the Word, and the Word was with God, and the Word was God. The same was in the beginning with God."* (John 1:1–2 NIV)

This is the incarnation—the real Christmas story. *"And the Word was made flesh, and dwelt among us..."* That's when Jesus came into this world. He became flesh. The word *dwelt* in the Greek language and coming from the Hebrew language could be literally translated he *tabernacled* amongst us.

If you've read your Old Testament, God spoke about being with His people. Eventually they had a temple, but first they had a tent, and then a tabernacle where rites and rituals foreshadowing the cross were performed. This tabernacle was mobile, but God was in the Holy of Holies. That was his presence.

What he is saying in John, chapter one is that Jesus, the Word made flesh, made his tabernacle with us and in us. We no longer need to go to a specific place to meet with God. He came to be with us. The Word "tabernacled" among us. It even gets better, because when you receive Him (John 1:12), you get power to become the sons of God. I don't have to go to a place to find God. I've received Christ. He lives in my heart.

Then we have this dynamic of the body, of the church, of the fellowship of believers. The house of the Lord refers to the house of the Lord in heaven. But it is not all for heaven. It is here also on earth.

David said, "I want to be in the house of the Lord all the days of my life on earth." Is the church the house of the Lord? Well, we are a habitation of God, but it's not about the building. God doesn't live in a local church building. He doesn't live in any building.

Some people think church buildings ought to look a certain way and ought to be ornate—like cathedrals. I go across Europe and other places and see big cathedrals. But nobody is there. You realize the real church is the people.

Listen to what the Apostle Paul says in Ephesians.

"Consequently, you are no longer foreigners and strangers, but fellow citizens…" That's a cool concept. *"…with God's people and also members of His household…"* We're part of his family. *"…built on the foundation of the apostles and prophets, with Christ Jesus Himself as the chief cornerstone. In Him the whole building* [the habitation, the household] *is joined together and rises to become a holy temple in the Lord."* (Ephesians 3:19–21 NIV)

That's us!

The house of the Lord is exponential when we are together. He goes on to say, *"And in Him you too are being built together to become a dwelling in which God lives by His Spirit."* That's the highest calling of the church, you see. When he says, "I want to dwell in the house of the Lord forever," you could literally say it this way. "Surely goodness and mercy shall follow me all the days of my life, and I will *continue* to dwell in the house of the Lord forever."

He is already in the house of the Lord. Eternity is now. Don't think of it as *now* and *later*. We're in eternity right now, so we should live by heavenly values. Have you ever heard the criticis, "Oh, he is so heavenly minded he is no earthly good"? It usually means someone is clueless, or a fanatic. Yet Paul said:

"Since, then, you have been raised with Christ, set your hearts on things above, where Christ is, seated at the right hand of God. Set your minds on things above, not on earthly things. For you died and your life is now hidden with Christ in God." (Colossians 3:1–2 NIV)

This is how we should think of our lives.

Eternity is now. Everybody here, everybody on earth, whether you're saved or lost, you're in eternity now. Not everybody has eternal life. There's a difference biblically between eternity and eternal life.

There's a difference between existence and life.

Eternal life is specifically related to those who have received and connected their life to the life of the eternal God. That's salvation.

The Simple Life

"For God so loved the world, that he gave his only begotten Son, that whosoever believeth in him should not perish, but have everlasting [or eternal] *life."* (John 3:16 NIV)

That's *salvation*.

A while back Karen and I were in Florida. Our hotel room had a wonderful view of the Gulf of Mexico. Karen loves to look at sunsets. She said, "I have to see the sunset!" I wanted to say, "They have one every night. Why don't you tell me when there is *not* going to be a sunset. That would be news!" But I bit my tongue and watched the sun sink below the horizon.

Just as sure as the sun goes down and the sun comes up, there are certain things that are going to happen.

One is that "goodness and mercy" follow believers all the days of life.

You say, "Well, what if I make a wrong turn?" He can fix that. It's like GPS in your car. On that trip to Florida, Karen booked us on a flight that left Dulles at 5:25 in the morning. *Left* Dulles at 5:25 in the morning. There is nobody at the airport at four o'clock in the morning.

We got on the flight. We were late leaving Dulles. We had a short window to make a connection in Charlotte. We got to Charlotte and thought we had just enough time. We raced through the airport. Well, Karen raced, and I followed far behind. We missed the connection.

David R. Stokes

There was a flight going to Fort Lauderdale, which would involve about a two-hour drive for us. Our final destination was Naples. So we flew down to Fort Lauderdale. We rented a car, and we had to drive through a section of the state called Alligator Alley.

I had a GPS. In the old days, if you got turned around, your wife would say, "Why don't you stop and ask directions?" No *real* man is going to do that. I told her that I was following the wisdom of Abraham. The Bible says Abraham and Sarah left their home and went not knowing where they were going. That's faith. The way to travel is by faith.

She said, "Well, you're no Abraham."

I decided not to reply. Instead I checked the GPS. It's awesome because if you start going the wrong way, it recalculates. It never says, "You cannot get there from here." It doesn't scold you. It just recalculates and gives you a new way to go.

In a sense that's how God leads us when we stray. God knows where you are. He is following. You're just dragging mercy and goodness along with you wherever you go. He recalculates, and He always has a way to get you back to where you should be.

"Surely goodness and mercy shall follow me all the days of my life…"

The Simple Life

Then I just take one more step, and I'm in the house of the Lord. I've been there all the time. Your best practice for heaven is to live like heaven on earth.

Now that's the simple life!

Acknowledgements

This short book flows from my preaching and teaching ministry. I am so grateful to all who gather at Expectation Church in Fairfax, Virginia, and who listen week after week to my talks.

I want to say a special word of thanks to my editorial assistant, Tracey Dowdy, for her help with this project. And I am also grateful to a wonderful group of "beta readers" for proofreading my prose: Al Donaldson, Holly Slater, Debby Stokes White, Tom Sleete, Howard "Ike" Hendershot, Kelly Ablaza, and many others who read at least part of the manuscript as it was being developed.

Special thanks to my son–in–law, Rev. Mike Zizolfo, for creating the cover for "The Simple Life."

And, as always, I couldn't do anything I do without the unwavering support of amazing my wife, Karen, and our daughters, Jennifer, Deborah, and Brenda.

David R. Stokes
Fairfax, Virginia
December 2015

About the Author

DAVID R. STOKES is a *Wall Street Journal* best-selling author. Three of his books are under review for development in Hollywood: "CAMELOT'S COUSIN: The Spy Who Betrayed Kennedy," "NOVEMBER SURPRISE" (sequel to "Camelot's Cousin"), and "CAPITOL LIMITED: The Forgotten First Kennedy & Nixon Debate in 1947." His first book, "THE SHOOTING SALVATIONIST: J. Frank Norris and the Murder Trial that Captivated America," a narrative nonfiction thriller and true crime bestseller, is also being considered as a six-part television miniseries.

An ordained minister since 1977, David speaks every Sunday (9:00 & 10:45 a.m.) at EXPECTATION CHURCH, a non-denominational ministry in Fairfax, Virginia, with more than 30 nations represented in its congregation.

He has hosted his own national satellite radio talk show and is a regular guest-host for talk shows around the country. David has also produced and hosted podcasts for The Cold War Museum and Richard Nixon Foundation.

David has been married to Karen since 1976 and they have three daughters and seven grandchildren. They live in beautiful Northern Virginia. His personal website is:

http://www.davidrstokes.com